"There are no secrets to success. It is the result of preparation, hard work, learning from failure."

— GENERAL COLIN POWELL

COLIN POWELL

By John Passaro

GRAPHIC DESIGN
Robert E. Bonaker / Graphic Design & Consulting Co.

PROJECT COORDINATOR
James R. Rothaus / James R. Rothaus & Associates

EDITORIAL DIRECTION
Elizabeth Sirimarco Budd

COVER PHOTO
Portrait of General Colin Powell / Schomburg Center for Research in Black Culture

Library of Congress Cataloging-in-Publication Data
Passaro, John, 1953-
Colin Powell / by John Passaro.
p. cm.
Summary: Surveys the life and military accomplishments
of Colin Powell, as well as his struggles
with racial prejudice.
ISBN 1-56766-619-1 (library : reinforced : alk. paper)

1. Powell, Colin L. — Juvenile literature. 2. Generals —
United States — Biography — Juvenile literature.
3. Afro-American generals — Biography — Juvenile literature.
4. United States — Army Biography — Juvenile literature.
[1. Powell, Colin L. — Juvenile literature. 2. Generals.
3. Afro-Americans — Biography] I. Title

E840.5.P68P37 1999
355'.0092 — dc21   99-19250
[B]   CIP

Contents

An Immigrant Family

In August 1990, Iraq invaded its southern neighbor, the country of Kuwait. Other nations believed this was wrong. Leaders around the world insisted that Iraq leave Kuwait. The Iraqi army refused to *retreat*. In January 1991, the *United Nations* (UN) declared war on Iraq. The *Persian Gulf War* had begun. In less than two months, Iraq *surrendered*. UN forces freed the country of Kuwait.

General Colin Powell played an important role in the Persian Gulf War. He helped U.S. President George Bush make some serious decisions. Americans respected Powell's skill and intelligence. Many even hoped he might run for president one day. Throughout his life, General Powell has achieved many goals. He believes his family helped him succeed.

Colin Powell's parents, Ariel and Luther, were both *immigrants* from Jamaica. Like many people, they came to the United States hoping to find better opportunities. They met at a party in their neighborhood in New York City. Soon they fell in love and married.

Private Collection of Colin Powell/Courtesy of Random House Publishers

COLIN POWELL'S MOTHER, ARIEL, IN 1924, WHEN SHE WAS 22 YEARS OLD.

COLIN AT AGE SEVEN WITH HIS FATHER, LUTHER POWELL. COLIN SAYS THE LOVE AND SUPPORT OF HIS FAMILY HELPED HIM ACHIEVE SUCCESS.

Private Collection of Colin Powell/Courtesy of Random House Publishers

AUTOMOBILES ARE ONE OF GENERAL POWELL'S
HOBBIES. EVEN AS A CHILD, THEY FASCINATED
HIM. "FROM THE DAY POP PULLED UP...
WITH A 1946 PONTIAC," COLIN WROTE IN
HIS AUTOBIOGRAPHY, "I BEGAN A LOVE AFFAIR
WITH CARS."

Ariel and Luther had a daughter named Marilyn in 1931. Colin was born five and a half years later on April 5, 1937. Ariel and Luther worked hard for their family. Both of them had jobs in a clothing factory. Ariel was a seamstress. Luther worked as a shipping clerk.

Private Collection of Colin Powell/Courtesy of Random House Publishers

The Powell family was not alone in New York. They had many relatives nearby. Many other Jamaicans lived in the city, too. They all helped one another like a big family. Some mothers put money into a group savings account. People in the community could borrow money in times of trouble. They could also use it to pay for their children's education. The neighborhood members called these shared funds *chetas*.

The Powells wanted their children to have a good education. Most of the people they knew in Jamaica did not even graduate from high school. In the United States, many Jamaican children went to college. Both Colin and Marilyn attended college. Then they continued their studies, and both earned a *masters degree*.

COLIN AND HIS SISTER MARILYN OUTSIDE THEIR APARTMENT IN NEW YORK CITY. AS A CHILD, COLIN SPENT MOST OF HIS TIME PLAYING WITH HIS FRIENDS AND FAMILY.

Colin Powell did not always have such big goals. His main interest in grade school was playing with his friends. Immigrants from many different countries lived in the Powell neighborhood. Children of all different colors and backgrounds played together every day. Instead of thinking about each other differently because of their skin colors, the children in Colin's neighborhood grew up without *prejudice*.

"Sweet Pea," as his family called Colin, did not earn the best grades in school. He graduated from Morris High School with a "C" average. Colin went on to college because his parents expected it of him. He did not want to disappoint them.

After Colin arrived at City College of New York, his life changed. He joined the Reserve Officers Training Corps (ROTC). ROTC prepares students for military service. After college, members of ROTC enter the military as *officers*.

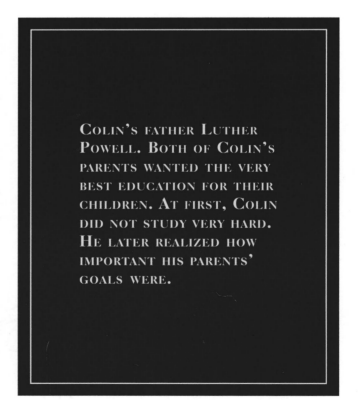

Private Collection of Colin Powell/Courtesy of Random House Publishers

COLIN'S FATHER LUTHER POWELL. BOTH OF COLIN'S PARENTS WANTED THE VERY BEST EDUCATION FOR THEIR CHILDREN. AT FIRST, COLIN DID NOT STUDY VERY HARD. HE LATER REALIZED HOW IMPORTANT HIS PARENTS' GOALS WERE.

Private Collection of Colin Powell/Courtesy of Random House Publishers

COLIN IN HIS FIRST ROTC UNIFORM. AFTER HE JOINED THE ROTC, COLIN KNEW THAT HE WANTED TO HAVE A CAREER IN THE MILITARY.

Private Collection of Colin Powell/Courtesy of Random House Publishers

COLIN NEVER LEFT NEW YORK CITY UNTIL HE JOINED THE ROTC. ONCE HE FINISHED COLLEGE, THE MILITARY SENT HIM ALL OVER THE WORLD.

Colin liked the discipline of the ROTC. He also liked the strong friendships he made with other ROTC members. He felt proud to wear the dark blue uniform with its shiny belt buckle, brass shirt buttons, and gold shoulder braids. Colin had finally found something he really wanted to do. Even today, he believes this was the key to his success. He found something he liked to do, then he worked very hard at it.

Colin was also very talented. He became the leader of his unit. He was also at the top of his class. One summer, he went to a ROTC training camp. The officers voted him the second-best *cadet*. It was the highest honor any black person had ever achieved at the camp. Then someone told him that if he were white, he would have been voted the best recruit of all. For the first time, Colin truly understood *discrimination*.

Powell was upset, but he kept a positive attitude. He also continued to succeed. At graduation, he held the rank of cadet colonel — the highest rank in the ROTC.

COLIN'S 1958 YEARBOOK PICTURE FROM CITY COLLEGE OF NEW YORK. COLIN SAYS HE FIRST BECAME INTERESTED IN THE MILITARY DURING COLLEGE.

Archive Photos/Swartz Collection

A Four-Star Superstar

After college, Colin Powell was sent to Georgia for the army's basic training. Colin had never been to the South before. He realized that *African Americans* were treated differently there. Even though black soldiers had the same rights as white people on the army base, they had to be careful in town. Off the base, African American people came face to face with *segregation*.

In the South, African Americans could not eat in the same restaurants as white people. They could not go to the same theaters. They could not stay in the same hotels or join the same clubs. In church, blacks sat in the balcony, away from whites. Drinking fountains and rest rooms were usually marked with signs saying "Whites Only" or "Colored Only." (African Americans were called "colored people" or "Negroes" at the time.) On public buses, blacks had to sit in the back seats, while whites sat in the front. If a bus were full, blacks had to give up their seats so that whites could sit.

Private Collection of Colin Powell/Courtesy of Random House

COLIN (FRONT ROW, RIGHT) WITH HIS ROTC CLASSMATES AT CITY COLLEGE OF NEW YORK. GENERAL POWELL AND THE OTHER CADETS HAVE STAYED FRIENDS OVER THE YEARS.

CORBIS-Bettmann

SEGREGATION LAWS AFFECTED MANY PARTS OF LIFE IN THE SOUTH.
THESE LAWS WERE MEANT TO KEEP BLACKS AND WHITES APART.

Colin was disappointed and hurt by such treatment. He knew it was wrong and refused to lower his opinion of himself. He also refused to change his goals. Colin Powell continued to believe in himself. He planned to make the most of his opportunities.

Colin was later sent to Fort Devens in Massachusetts. In 1961, he met a girl named Alma Johnson. Alma came from Alabama. Colin admired her soft voice and her pretty face. Even more important, Alma was a very intelligent woman. She worked as an *audiologist*.

She helped people who were hard of hearing. Colin and Alma began to spend a lot of time together. Soon they fell in love. On August 25, 1962, they were married.

A few months later, Colin learned that the army was sending him away. He was going to fight in the Vietnam War. North Vietnam was trying to conquer South Vietnam. The United States decided to help South Vietnam.

Alma moved to Alabama to live with her parents. Powell arrived in Vietnam on Christmas morning 1962. At first, he was excited to fight for the United States. It seemed like the first adventure of his military career.

Private Collection of Colin Powell/Courtesy of Random House Publishers

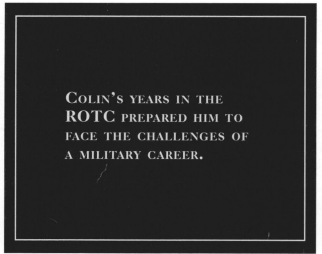

COLIN'S YEARS IN THE ROTC PREPARED HIM TO FACE THE CHALLENGES OF A MILITARY CAREER.

Private Collection of Colin Powell/Courtesy of Random House Publishers

COLIN MARRIED ALMA JOHNSON ON AUGUST 25, 1962.
COLIN'S PARENTS ARE STANDING NEXT TO ALMA, AND THE
JOHNSONS ARE NEXT TO COLIN.

His assignment stopped being an adventure a few weeks later. During his first night in battle, Colin heard the crack of real gun shots. He saw live bullets fly past him. War was no longer a fun game. Instead, it was frightening and sad.

The battle was over in just a few moments. Colin Powell heard screaming. There was confusion.

When he went to help, he saw one soldier lying dead on the ground. Many others were wounded.

The soldier's death had a powerful effect on Colin. The next morning, he felt happy to be alive. He also felt guilty that he had survived when someone in his group had died.

Private Collection of Colin Powell/Courtesy of Random House Publishers

COLIN IN 1963, DURING HIS FIRST TRIP TO VIETNAM. AT FIRST, COLIN WAS EXCITED TO FIGHT FOR HIS COUNTRY. AS TIME WENT ON, HE REALIZED THAT WAR WAS A SAD AND TERRIBLE THING.

Private Collection of Colin Powell/Courtesy of Random House Publishers

IN 1968, POWELL RETURNED TO VIETNAM. HE, HIS GENERAL, AND A FEW
SOLDIERS WERE INVOLVED IN A HELICOPTER CRASH IN VIETNAM. THIS PICTURE
WAS TAKEN SHORTLY AFTER THE ACCIDENT. POWELL (RIGHT) AND ANOTHER
SOLDIER BRAVELY PULLED THE OTHER PASSENGERS FROM THE WRECKAGE.
EVERYONE SURVIVED, BUT THE PILOT WAS BADLY HURT.

THE POWELL FAMILY IN 1975. ALMA AND COLIN HAVE THREE CHILDREN (FROM LEFT TO RIGHT), ANNE MARIE, LINDA, AND MICHAEL.

Colin returned to Alabama in 1963. He had hoped that discrimination and prejudice were gone, but Colin was soon disappointed. Life was still difficult for blacks in the South. One night, Colin went to a restaurant to get something to eat. He knew he couldn't go into the restaurant because he was black. Waiters also served people in their cars. Colin decided to try that. After a long wait, a worker finally came to his car. She asked him if he was Puerto Rican. Colin said he wasn't. She asked him if he was one of the African soldiers studying on the army base. Colin said he wasn't an African. He was an American.

The worker seemed uncomfortable. She said she couldn't serve him. She offered to pass him a hamburger through the back door. Colin told her he wasn't *that* hungry. He saw white customers inside the restaurant laughing as he drove away. Colin went back to the army base where he could be served like everyone else.

In 1964, Colin returned to the same restaurant. This time, things were different. President Lyndon B. Johnson had signed the Civil Rights Act. This law made it illegal to discriminate against anyone in a public place. Now no one could refuse service to a black person.

Four years later, the army sent Colin back to Vietnam. The excitement he felt the first time he went to war was gone. The Powells now had three children, Michael, Linda, and Anne Marie. Colin was worried about leaving his young family. It was a difficult time in the United States as well. The war was not going well. Many Americans were against it. Even the U.S. government seemed unsure of its role in the war. Even so, Powell still did the best job he could. He was proud to serve his country.

When the war was over, all the soldiers came home. In the past, Americans treated soldiers like heroes. Now people ignored or even criticized Vietnam *veterans*. People complained about the military as well. Because of this poor treatment and their difficult memories of the war, many soldiers left the military.

CORBIS/Wally McNamee

VIETNAM VETERANS HAD A VERY DIFFICULT TIME DURING THE WAR. THEN WHEN THEY RETURNED TO THE UNITED STATES, MANY PEOPLE TREATED THEM POORLY.

Colin Powell decided to stay in the army. He still believed in the military. The army recognized Powell's dedication. It sent him back to school to study for a masters degree. After earning his degree, Colin spent a year working at the White House. Then he returned to his regular military duties.

Over time, Colin rose higher and higher in rank. In 1978, he became a brigadier general. The army gave him many important assignments. Sometimes he was sent to command troops. Other times, he worked with leaders in Washington, D.C.

President Ronald Reagan recognized Powell's talent. In 1987, he asked Powell to be his national security assistant. Powell became the first African American four-star general. In 1989, General Powell received another honor. He became the *chairman* of the *Joint Chiefs of Staff*. General Powell was now the most important military advisor to the new president, George Bush.

CORBIS-Bettmann

COLIN POWELL WITH PRESIDENT RONALD REAGAN AND OTHER WHITE HOUSE STAFF MEMBERS. PRESIDENT REAGAN ASKED COLIN TO BE HIS NATIONAL SECURITY ASSISTANT. GENERAL POWELL BECAME THE HIGHEST RANKING AFRICAN AMERICAN IN THE U.S. ARMY.

Archive Photos/Consolidated News

GENERAL POWELL MET WITH THE FOREIGN MINISTER OF KUWAIT IN 1990. THEY DISCUSSED HOW THE UNITED STATES COULD HELP KUWAIT AFTER THE IRAQI INVASION.

The Persian Gulf War

On August 2, 1990, the Iraqi army invaded Kuwait. Kuwait is a tiny country, but it has a huge supply of oil within its borders. It supplies about 20 percent of the world's oil. Iraq wanted to control this valuable resource. The rest of the world was very worried. What would happen to the people of Kuwait? What would happen if Iraq controlled so much oil?

President Bush met with all of his advisors, including General Powell. The president decided Iraq must leave Kuwait. Military force might be needed to accomplish this. General Powell believed that countries should always avoid war. If war cannot be avoided, then the United States should do everything it can to win. President Bush agreed with Powell.

The United States joined forces with other members of the United Nations. They decided to give Iraq a deadline to leave Kuwait: January 15th, 1991. In order to prepare for the deadline, 28 countries sent troops to the Persian Gulf. More than 40 other nations supported the effort.

GENERAL POWELL DURING A VISIT TO THE PERSIAN GULF.

The deadline passed, but Iraq still refused to leave Kuwait. The time had come to start the war. General Norman Schwarzkopf of the United States Army was in charge of all the troops, even those from other nations. Early in the morning on January 17th, the attack began.

For more than one month, aircraft bombed military targets in Iraq. The Iraqis still would not leave Kuwait. General Powell said it was time to send ground troops to the area. Soldiers would march into Kuwait and force out the Iraqi army. The president agreed.

On February 24, General Schwarzkopf began the attack. In less than 72 hours, the Iraqis were driven out of Kuwait. UN forces killed many Iraqi soldiers. They also destroyed much of the Iraqi army's equipment. By March 2, they had defeated Iraq. The next day, General Schwarzkopf met with the Iraqi generals. He accepted their surrender.

Both General Schwarzkopf and General Powell became well known because of their role in the Persian Gulf War. Many people considered them heroes. After the war, Powell continued to serve on the Joint Chiefs of Staff until he retired from the military in 1993.

CORBIS/Robin Adshead; The Military Picture Library

U.S. SOLDIERS EXAMINE AN IRAQI TANK DESTROYED DURING BATTLE. UN FORCES RUINED MUCH OF THE IRAQI ARMY'S EQUIPMENT DURING THE PERSIAN GULF WAR.

GENERAL POWELL AND GENERAL SCHWARZKOPF HAVE KNOWN EACH OTHER FOR A LONG TIME. SOMETIMES THEY DISAGREED ABOUT HOW TO SOLVE PROBLEMS DURING THE PERSIAN GULF WAR. STILL, THE TWO MEN ALWAYS RESPECTED EACH OTHER'S ABILITIES.

CORBIS/Jacques M. Chenet

IT TOOK GENERAL POWELL TWO YEARS TO WRITE HIS AUTOBIOGRAPHY. THE BOOK BECAME A BEST SELLER. MANY PEOPLE WANTED TO READ ABOUT HIS LIFE.

An American Journey

After his retirement, Powell spent two years writing his *autobiography*. He published *My American Journey* in September 1995. Powell visited book stores in 25 cities across the United States to autograph his book. Many old friends came to see him.

In his book, Powell tells readers about his career in the military. He discusses the Vietnam War and his experiences there. He wrote a chapter about the Persian Gulf War as well. Many people enjoy reading about his life.

Some people also find the book inspiring. General Powell tells readers that they can achieve almost anything if they work hard. He hopes his success will encourage other African Americans to have big goals. "My career," writes Powell, "should serve as a model to fellow blacks, in or out of the military, in demonstrating the possibilities of American life." Powell also knows that some white people are still prejudiced. He hopes his success will make them rethink their views.

CORBIS/Matthew Mendelson

GENERAL POWELL SPEAKS TO AN AUDIENCE BEFORE AUTOGRAPHING COPIES OF HIS BOOK. HE SIGNED EXACTLY 60,001 COPIES OF HIS BOOK, *MY AMERICAN JOURNEY.*

There may be another great achievement in store for Colin Powell. Many people believe he could become the first African American president. Powell decided not to run for president in 1996. He said, "I have spent long hours talking with my wife and children, the most important people in my life, about the impact an entry into political life would have on us. It would require sacrifices and changes in our lives that would be difficult for us to make at this time. The welfare of my family had to be uppermost in my mind."

The Powell family decided together that the time was not right. Alma and Colin had been married for 33 years. They had moved more than two dozen times. Things had finally calmed down after General Powell's retirement. He had more time to spend with his family.

No one knows if Powell will run for president someday. He will make the decision the same way he makes all important decisions. He starts by getting the facts. Then he thinks about them very carefully. Finally, he makes his decision.

THE BUFFALO SOLDIERS

AMERICAN VETERANS AMVETS OF WORLD WAR II KOREA VIET NAM

★ ★ ★ ★

N L. POWELL

CORBIS/Jacques M. Chenet

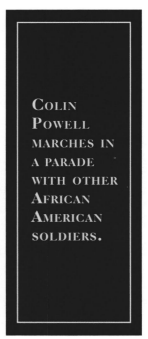

COLIN POWELL MARCHES IN A PARADE WITH OTHER AFRICAN AMERICAN SOLDIERS.

Archive Photos/Consolidated News

COLIN POWELL AND HIS WIFE ALMA ANNOUNCE THAT HE
WILL NOT RUN FOR PRESIDENT. POWELL TOLD REPORTERS,
"I KNOW THAT THIS IS THE RIGHT DECISION FOR ME."

Reuters/Gary Cameron/Archive Photos

GENERAL POWELL SPOKE AT THE PRESIDENT'S SUMMIT FOR AMERICA'S FUTURE. THE EVENT WAS HELD IN PHILADELPHIA DURING APRIL 1997. PRESIDENT BILL CLINTON ORGANIZED THE SUMMIT TO HELP AMERICAN YOUTH.

Many U.S. presidents were military heroes. The first general to follow this path was George Washington. He earned the nation's respect during the American Revolution. He became the new country's first president.

Ulysses S. Grant was a general of the Union Army during the American Civil War. He became the 26th president of the United States. General Dwight D. Eisenhower served in World War II. He came home a war hero, and Americans elected him president twice. Colin Powell has a long way to travel before he can follow in their footsteps. Becoming president is difficult for anyone to achieve. Some people believe a black candidate could not win an election. This would not stop Powell from trying. In fact, it may encourage him to prove what he can do.

In the meantime, Powell has traded his military uniform for a suit and tie. He is the chairman of a group called America's Promise. This organization believes children need five things to be successful. First, they need a caring adult or a mentor. Second, they need a safe place to go after school where they can learn and grow. Third, children must have a healthy start. Fourth, children need a good education. Finally, children need a chance to give something back to their communities.

Powell has recruited many large companies to help America's Promise. Some companies give free medicine and shots to children. Some donate nutritious food. Other companies have donated computers to schools.

What will the future hold for Colin Powell? Whatever he chooses to do, he will work hard to accomplish his goals. He will work with dedication and intelligence. He will put forth his best effort.

Colin Powell believes a good family is the most important ingredient for success. There are many different kinds of families. A Gulf War soldier once said his fellow soldiers were like family. They would all take care of each other, so he was not afraid to go to war. Colin Powell says that the citizens of the United States are also part of a big family. Americans can accomplish almost anything when they work together.

Archive Photos/Victor Malafronte

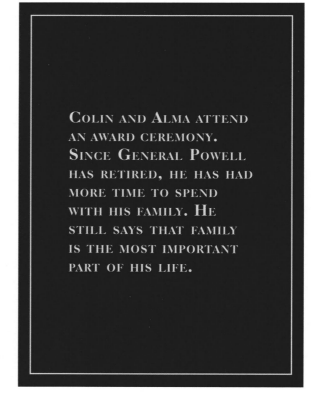

COLIN AND ALMA ATTEND AN AWARD CEREMONY. SINCE GENERAL POWELL HAS RETIRED, HE HAS HAD MORE TIME TO SPEND WITH HIS FAMILY. HE STILL SAYS THAT FAMILY IS THE MOST IMPORTANT PART OF HIS LIFE.

Reuters/Jim Bourg/Archive Photos

COLIN POWELL RECEIVES THOUSANDS OF REQUESTS TO SPEAK TO AUDIENCES EACH YEAR. MANY PEOPLE FIND HIS LIFE STORY INSPIRING.

Timeline

1937	Colin Powell is born in New York City on April 5.		*1978*	Powell is promoted to the rank of brigadier general.
1954	Powell joins the Reserve Officers Training Corps (ROTC).		*1987*	President Ronald Reagan appoints Powell as assistant to the president for national security affairs.
1958	Powell graduates from City College of New York. He enters the U.S. Army as a second lieutenant.		*1989*	President George Bush names Powell chairman of the Joint Chiefs of Staff.
1961	Powell meets his future wife, Alma Vivian Johnson.		*1991*	The Persian Gulf War takes place. The Iraqi army is defeated in less than two months.
1962	Alma and Colin Powell marry in August. In December, Colin Powell is sent to fight in the Vietnam War.		*1993*	Powell retires from the U.S. Army.
1968-1969	Powell returns to Vietnam for a second time.		*1995*	Powell publishes his book, *My American Journey*.
1971	Powell earns a masters degree.		*1996*	Powell decides not to run for president.
1972	Powell accepts his first job at the White House.			

Glossary

African Americans
(AF-ri-kan uh-MAYR-ih-kanz)
African Americans are black Americans whose ancestors came from Africa long ago. Colin Powell is an African American.

audiologist
(awd-ee-AWL-uh-jest)
An audiologist is a doctor that helps people with hearing problems. Alma Powell was an audiologist.

autobiography
(ott-oh-by-AWG-raf-ee)
An autobiography is a book that someone writes about him or herself. Colin Powell wrote his autobiography, *My American Journey*.

cadet
(ka-DET)
A cadet is a young soldier who is in training for the military.

chairman
(CHAIR-man)
A chairman is a person who serves as the head of an organization. General Colin Powell was the chairman of the Joint Chiefs of Staff.

discrimination
(dis-krim-ih-NAY-shun)
Discrimination is the unfair treatment of people simply because they are different. African Americans have suffered discrimination by whites.

immigrants
(IM-ih-grentz)
Immigrants are people who leave their native country to live somewhere else. Colin Powell's parents were immigrants from Jamaica.

Joint Chiefs of Staff
(JOYNT CHEEFZ of STAF)
The Joint Chiefs of Staff are military advisors to the president of the United States. General Colin Powell was the chairman of the Joint Chiefs of Staff during the Persian Gulf War.

masters degree
(MAS-turz duh-GREE)
A masters degree is a diploma given to people who continue their studies after college. Colin Powell and his sister Marilyn both earned masters degrees.

Glossary

officers
(OFF-eh-serz)
Officers are people in the military who are in charge of the troops. Members of ROTC are trained to be officers after they finish school.

Persian Gulf War
(PUR-zhen GULF WOR)
The Persian Gulf War took place during the first three months of 1991. United Nations forces, led by the United States, fought against Iraq to free the country of Kuwait.

prejudice
(PREJ-uh-des)
Prejudice is a negative feeling or opinion about someone without a good reason. Black Americans have often faced prejudice from whites.

retreat
(ree-TREET)
If an army retreats, they leave some place. The Iraqi army refused to retreat from Kuwait.

segregation
(seg-rih-GAY-shun)
Segregation is actions and laws that separate people from one another. Blacks and whites were segregated in the South for many years.

surrender
(suh-REN-dur)
If someone surrenders, they give up. The Iraqi army surrendered to United Nations forces after the Persian Gulf War.

United Nations (yoo-NYT-ed NAY-shuns)
The United Nations (UN) is an international organization made up of 185 countries. UN members attempt to solve world problems by working together.

veterans (VET-eh-ranz)
Veterans are people who were once in the military. Colin Powell is a veteran of the United States Army.

Index

For Further Information

Books

King, John. *The Gulf War.* Minneapolis, MN: Dillon Press, 1991.

Landau, Elaine. *Colin Powell: Four Star General.* New York: Franklin Watts, 1991.

Brown, Gene. *The Nation in Turmoil: Civil Rights and the Vietnam War (1960 – 1973).* Brookfield, CT: Twenty-first Century Books, 1995.

Web Sites

Read an on-line interview with General Colin Powell:
http://www.achievement.org/
After arriving at the site, go to the Gallery of Achievement and then to the Hall of Public Service.

Learn more about the Persian Gulf War:
http://www.desert-storm.com/

Learn about other African American soldiers:
http://www.abest.com/~cklose/aawar.htm

Visit the Library of Congress site about African Americans:
http://lcweb.loc.gov/exhibits/african/afam001.html